The Spell of Being

SHRUTI ANAND

I dedicate this book to Lord Shiva, Lord Hanuman, my guarding light, my protector and my constant. It is with your divine blessings that I have written this book.

To my maternal grandparents, thank you for your unconditional love, you are forever in my heart.

Contents

1. Inkling Of Love 2

2. Déjà vu 4

3. The Tidal Waves.. 6

4. The Digital Era.. 8

5. Who Is It In The Mirror? 10

6. The Journey Of Life 12

7. I am Dreaming 14

8. Riddle Of Time 16

9. The Staircase.. 18

10. Puddles Of Memories 20

11. Lost In The Whispering Woods............................ 22

12. The Blooming Heart.. 24

ABOUT THE AUTHOR 26

Fig 1

1. Inkling Of Love

Oh how wonderful is that YOU & I see the same world
...

Our hearts connected by an invisible thread, a presence felt by the two of us…

They ask me what is love? Oh such an irony, I haven't fallen in love yet, but I firmly believe you exist somewhere…

You carry a piece of my heart. I see a blurry face in my dreams…

So how will I recognize you? In heaps of people you will seize my heart like no one else.

Fig 2

2. Déjà vu

I walked into an art gallery, the display of pictures absolutely mesmerized me, but I was enticed by a particular piece of art…

I felt I have seen it before, tried recollecting, looked around & suddenly the entire place seemed familiar…

.

The voices around me gradually fading away & me trying to figure out this feeling? Was I drifting into the past?

Have I lived a life before this or am I living another life simultaneously in another time zone?

Fig 3

3. The Tidal Waves

I sit near the shore looking for answers, the tides have come & gone…

The ripples in the sea creating a pattern, as if someone is talking to me…

Time has taken a spiral turn, but here I am searching for the final dot.

Fig 4

4. The Digital Era

We are moving from one App to another, juggling between likes, follow & comments...

The numbers give us a high , momentary happiness or is it everyone seeking validation?

The person in the trending video gets noticed by millions, but in a few days he is also forgotten,. The attention span is becoming shorter & shorter...

Its easy to connect with anyone around the world but even more difficult to communicate...

We don't have time to be bored, as there are multiple options to explore. The likes & the number of followers get noticed but the meaningful captions get pushed behind...

We no more live in a house, we are living in digital squares.

Fig 5

5. Who Is It In The Mirror?

Its not 'YOU' looking yourself in the mirror…

There is something beyond this…

Look within yourself & you will reaize who is the one between the 'REAL' & the 'ABSTRACT'…

The deep, twisted & unfathomable symbolization of the mirror…

Carve out time for 'REFLECTION' .

Fig 6

6. The Journey Of Life

Life is like a train journey & we all are travellers in this journey called life…

Some people travel light, while some carry a baggage of emotions with them..

As one peeps out of the window, the stations pass by like a whirlwind, so is the time always running out…

The more one tries to catch hold the visual of a station, the more it will be left behind…

The passengers in the train are strangers but they do become our companion for a brief interval of time, each one of them having a story of their own…

The tales of happiness, memories, success, sorrow & struggle..

Oh how wonderful is that everyone is connected with the same dot & the train journey has the same destination.

Fig 7

7. I am Dreaming

I lie down after a long day..

The events of the day rushing through my head. Slowly dozing off, amidst two parallel worlds, one in which I am currently taking rest & the one in which I am stepping into…

.

I drift into an undiscovered world, slowly being engulfed by the white clouds, as if they are playing hide & seek with me…

I look down & find myself standing on top of the cliff…as far as I can see, I am surrounded by valleys, so alluring…

The mountainas are humoungous, I feel tiny & all of a sudden I hear a voice "The valleys are a depiction of the courage within you" …

I look around & there is not a soul. I decide to take a leap onto the other mountain & I wake up from my slumber.

fig 8

8. Riddle Of Time

One day all the pieces of the puzzle will come together…

One day everything will become seamless, no comma's, no ifs, no full stops…

One day things will magically unfold in front of your eyes…

It has started to rain & the rainbow is just round the corner.

Fig 9

9. The Staircase

A staircase to the unexplained..

Deep mysteries unraveled…

Where humans walk free..

Like a tree that sheds it's leaves..

No masks & no guards up.

Fig 10

10. Puddles Of Memories

Sitting by the window, on a bright sunny day,

I saw a man passing by..

The sweet memories of childhood came rushing back…

The colourful Popsicles stacked up, the musical sound of the bell on the cart, captivating all the kids..

Like the river that flows through the rocks, the kids came gushing out..

And in a minute the cart was bustling with 'LiFe' .

Fig 11

11. Lost In The Whispering Woods

She came to the forest and the sun rose above the horizon each day for her…..

It came out like a beaming glow ball shining upon her…

She sat somewhere in the middle of the forest to meet him…

She was the shy girl, not the timid one, but the 'magical one'. Couldn't look him in the eye but everytime he looked at her she became pink in the face.

12. The Blooming Heart

The garden of love , where the butterflies grow..

The fireflies glow & the flowers bloom…

The soft wind blows & the flowers start dancing, creating a symphony…

What turns out, is a visual delight which made the little turtle come out of its shell.

ABOUT THE AUTHOR

Shruti Anand is a lifestyle content creator with an engineering and management academic background, brought up in the city beautiful Chandigarh. She knows the art of transforming dreams into reality. She loves dancing , music and travelling. She has an inclination towards developing new skills. She practices yoga and meditation holistically and believes these are the grounds for a fulfilling life.

Social Media Handles

Instagram – shrutianand01

Youtube- Shruti Anand (Handle- shrutianand9)

Facebook- Wardrobe & Fitness

Email - shrutianand4@gmail.com

www.ingramcontent.com/pod-product-compliance
Lightning Source LLC
Chambersburg PA
CBHW021156130726
47988CB00004B/1643

The radioactive machine

This is the third book in the series of the various books that the author has written in the attempt to answer some of the unanswered mysteries in the field of space, science and the cosmos. In the last book the main topic of consideration was the man made wormholes or transversable wormholes, in this book a lot of new information regarding these structures was given like the ways a black hole may make combinations with other black holes and the white holes, the number of these wormholes formed, and lastly we also discussed about a formula which will help us to create a wormhole based on any kind of mass that we desire.

Now in this particular book the main target of consideration will be a new kind of machine which if invented and created will help the humanity a lot.

Now a question arises why this machine and what is the need of it, what will it help in? What will be its basic work mechanism? What fuel will it use?

In order to answer these many questions lets straight ahead jump into the main contents of the book and there the best effort will be put to answer all these questions and introduce new equipment in the field where we are all trying to work and find some mysterious answers.

Table of contents

Chapter 1 Introduction

.... (3-4)

Chapter 2 the main machine

.... (5-16)

Chapter 3 The moscrovium problem

.... (16-17)